SWEDEN

Discover Sweden Culture, Sports, History, Cuisine, Landmarks, People, Traditions, and many more for Kids

LOCATION

North - Finland, Norway

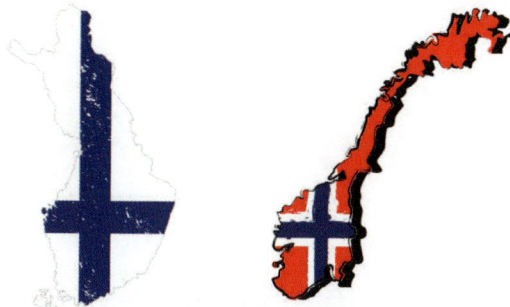

West - Norway

East- Baltic Sea, Gulf of Bothnia

South - Denmark

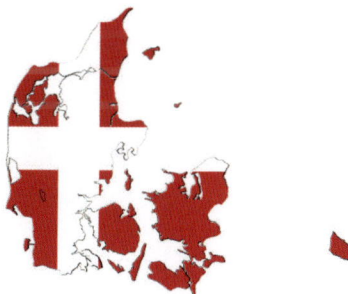

POPULATION

10.4 Million

China population

1425 Million

India Population
1428 Million

CLIMATE

Sweden experiences a temperate climate with four distinct seasons

Wet season

Dry season

July and August

February and March

NATIONAL DAY

June 6th,1523

From

Danish Rule

MOTTO > "För Sverige – i tiden" Means
"For Sweden – With the Times"

CAPITAL

Stockholm

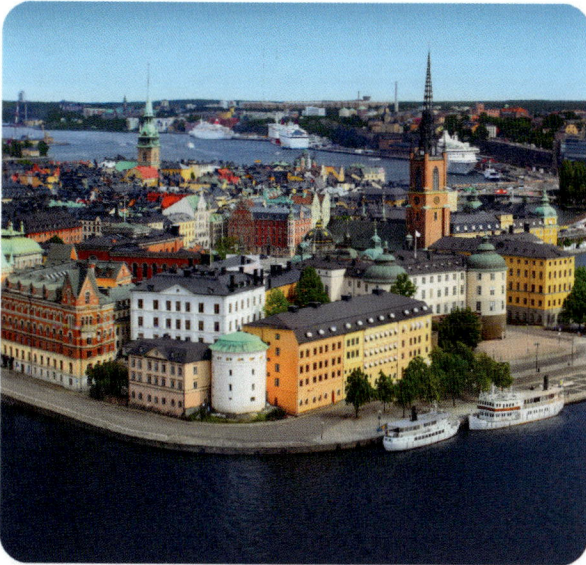

- Stockholm is built on 14 islands.

- It has a famous amusement park called Gröna Lund.

- The city has more than 50 bridges connecting the islands.

- It hosts the Nobel Prize ceremonies.

- The Vasa Museum has a 17th-century ship that sank and was recovered.

CURRENCY

Swedish Krona (SEK)

Denominations notes

20, 50, 100, 200, 500, 1000 kronor

Coins - 1, 2, 5, 10 kronor

LANGUAGE

GOTT NYTT ÅR

Official Language

FiKA?

SWEDISH

EDUCATION

Compulsory education from ages 7 to 16, with public and private schools available. Emphasizes creativity and critical thinking.

NATIONAL FLAG

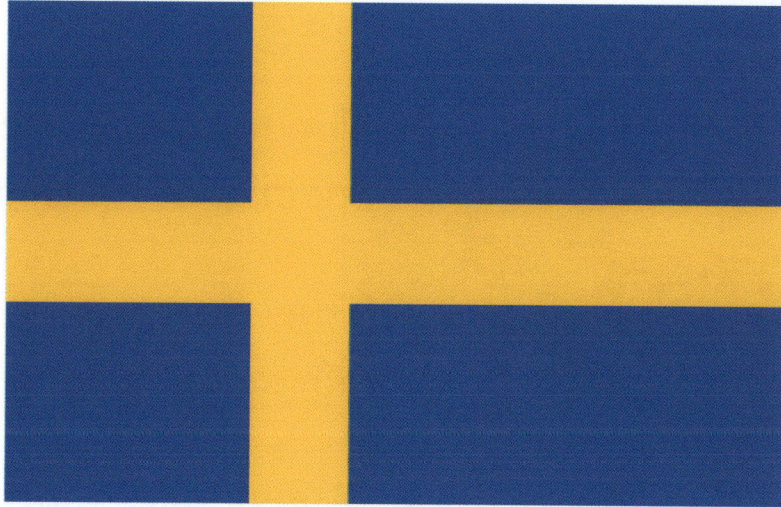

- The blue represents loyalty, truth, and justice.

- The yellow or gold cross symbolizes generosity and the light of the sun.

NATIONAL ANIMAL

Eurasian Elk (Moose)

- The moose is the largest species of deer in the world.

- They have large antlers that can span up to 6 feet.

- Moose are good swimmers and can dive up to 6 meters.

- They eat plants, leaves, and twigs.

- Moose are often seen in Swedish forests.

NATIONAL BIRD

Eurasian Blackbird

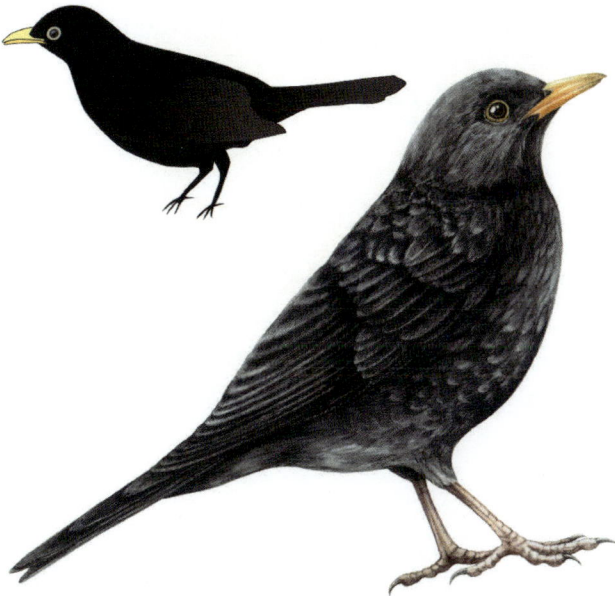

- Blackbirds are known for their beautiful singing.

- They are common in gardens and forests.

- Male blackbirds are black with a yellow beak, while females are brown.

- They eat insects, berries, and worms.

- Blackbirds build nests in trees or bushes.

NATIONAL TREE

Silver Birch

- The Silver Birch has white bark that peels in layers.

- It is commonly found in Swedish forests.

- Birch trees can grow up to 25 meters tall.

- They produce catkins, which are long flower clusters.

- The wood is used for making furniture and paper.

NATIONAL FLOWER

Twinflower

- The Twinflower is named after Carl Linnaeus, a famous Swedish botanist.

- It has small pinkish-white flowers.

- It is found in cool, moist forests.

- The flowers grow in pairs, hence the name "Twinflower."

- The plant has a pleasant, sweet fragrance.

TRADITIONAL MEDICINE

1) Chamomile

- Used to treating insomnia, anxiety, and to soothe stomach ailments and menstrual cramps.

2) Arnica

- Used to treat treat bruises, sprains, and muscle pain.

3) Bilberry

- Supports eye health, helps with diarrhea, and boosts circulation.

4) Yarrow

- Used for wound healing, digestive issues, and reducing fever.

BEAUTIFUL BEACHES

There are over 100 beaches in Sweden

Skanör Beach

Tofta Beach

Pite Havsbad

Sudersand Beach

Tylösand Beach

Ribersborg Beach

NATIONAL PARK

There are 30 National parks in Sweden

Abisko National Park

Sarek National Park

Stora Sjöfallet National Park

Padjelanta National Park

Tyresta National Park

Fulufjället National Park

LAND MARKS

Stockholm Palace

Drottningholm Palace

Vasa Museum

Icehotel

Gamla Stan (Old Town)

Liseberg

LAND MARKS

Öresund Bridge

Kiruna Church

Kalmar Castle

Kungsleden

Storkyrkan

Uppsala Cathedral

ECONOMY

Based on

Forestry

Pharmaceuticals

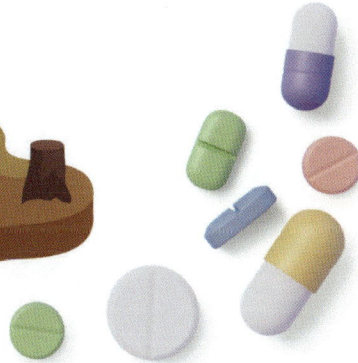

Information Technology

IT

Manufacturing (automobiles, machinery)

Telecommunications

EXPORTS

Automobiles

Paper products

Machinery and equipment

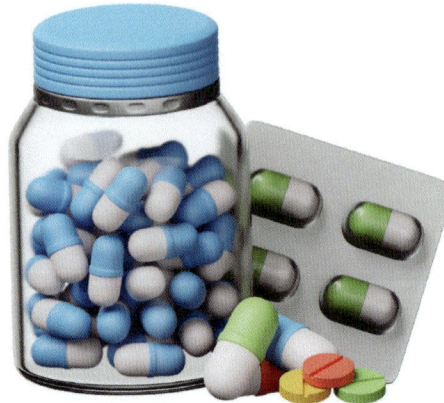

Pharmaceuticals

Iron and steel

WILD LIFE

Eco system most diverse in the world

Moose

Reindeer

Lynx

Brown Bear

Wolf

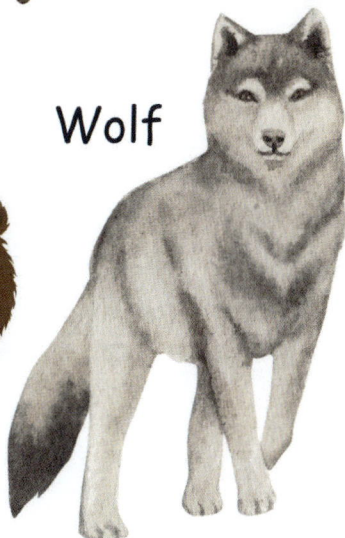

European Bison

MARINE LIFE

Eco system most diverse in the world

Atlantic Salmon

Cod

Herring

Pike

Perch

Mackerel

Flounder

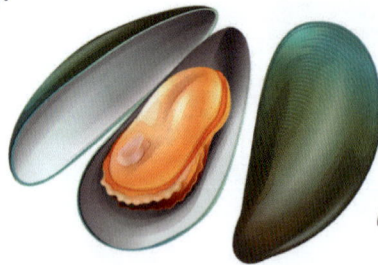

Mussels

BIRDS & BUTTERFLY

Paradise for birds watchers

More than 500 Species

122 Butterfly varierty

SPORTS & ADVENTURES

Popular Sports are as follows

Soccer

Hiking

Sailing

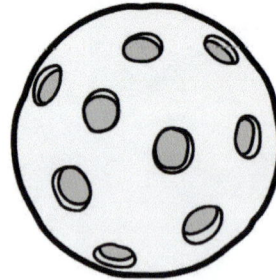

Floorball

Ice hockey

Mountain biking

Cross-country skiing

FAMOUS PEOPLE

Alfred Nobel
(Inventor of Dynamite
and founder of the
Nobel Prizes_

Astrid Lindgren
(Author)

Greta Thunberg
(Environmental Activist)

Zlatan Ibrahimović
(Footballer)

ABBA
(Famous pop group)

ARTS & CRAFTS

Dalahäst

Glass art

Sami handicrafts
(duodji)

Swedish pottery

Textile
Arts

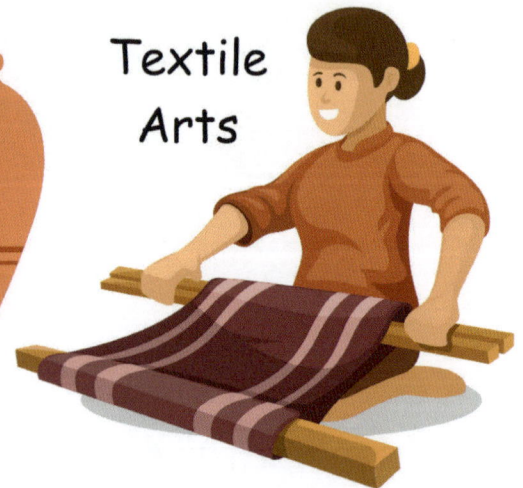

CUISINE

Country has multi cultural society

Meatballs	Gravlax	Lingonberry jam	Crispbread

Cinnamon buns	Smörgåsbord	Pea soup	Surströmming

Swedish pancakes	Västerbotten cheese	Raggmunk

FESTIVALS

Midsummer

Walpurgis Night

Lucia Day

Crayfish Party

Christmas

MUSIC INSTRUMENTS

Nyckelharpa

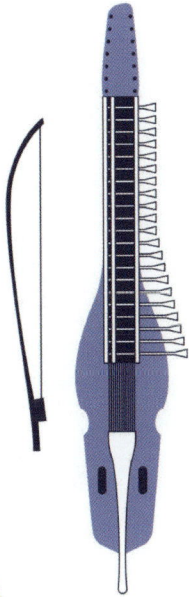

Accordion

Fiddle

Guitar

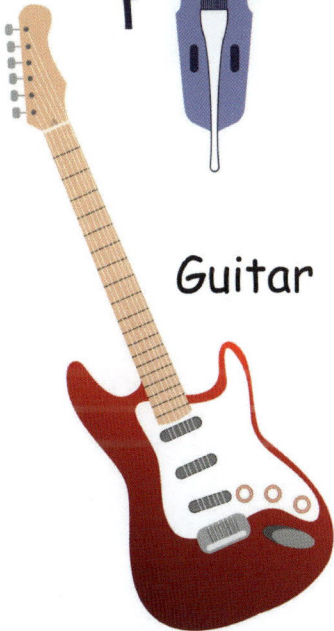

Piano

Recorder

UNESCO- WORLD HERITAGE SITES

There are 15 UNESCO sites in Sweden

Drottningholm Palace

Birch and Djurgården

Engelsberg Ironworks

Rock Carvings in Tanum

Skogskyrkogården

Grimeton Radio Station

INTERNATIONAL RELATIONS

European Union

United Nations

- Member of the European Union

- Active in the United Nations

- Promotes human rights and democracy

- Strong ties with Nordic countries

- Supports global environmental sustainability

FUN FACTS

- Sweden is one of the largest countries in Europe.

- Sweden is known for its high standard of living.

- Northern Lights

- In the north of Sweden, you can see the Northern Lights, a colorful display in the sky.

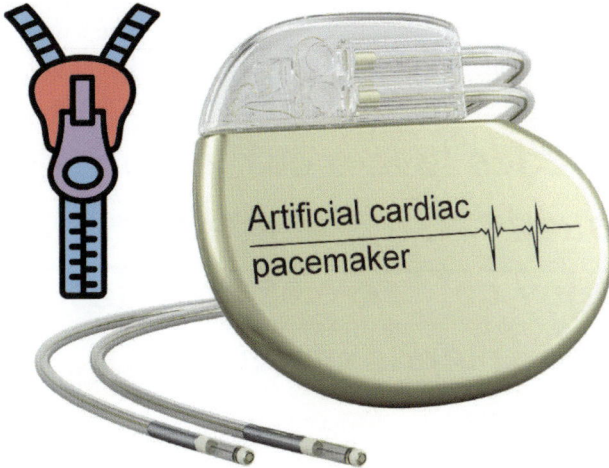

Inventive Country

- Sweden is the birthplace of many famous inventions, including the pacemaker and the zipper.

Artificial cardiac pacemaker

Midnight Sun

- During the summer, the sun never sets above the Arctic Circle in Sweden.

- **Fika lovers**

- Swedes love a coffee break called "fika," where they enjoy coffee and pastries with friends or family.

- **Recycling Champions**

- Sweden is so good at recycling that it imports waste from other countries to recycle.

- **The Nobel Prizes**

- The Nobel Prizes in physics, chemistry, medicine, literature, and peace were founded by Swedish inventor Alfred Nobel.

- **Many Lakes**

- There are nearly 100,000 lakes in Sweden, big and small.

- Very Old Town

- The town of Ystad in Sweden has buildings that date back to the 11th century.

- Longest Art Gallery

- The Stockholm metro is considered the world's longest art gallery, with art in nearly every station.

Cashless Society

- Sweden is one of the countries leading the move towards becoming a cashless society, where very few people use cash.

Dala Horse

- A traditional carved, painted wooden horse statuette is a popular Swedish souvenir.

- **Allemansrätten**
- This is a law that allows people to freely explore nature, including private lands, without disturbing or destroying.

- **Unique Easter Tradition**
- Children dress up as Easter witches, wearing old and discarded clothes.

Printed in Dunstable, United Kingdom

65692087R00025